THE PUPPET MASTER

By

LaShonda Hunter-Perera

ACKNOWLEDGMENTS

Thank you for your guidance and support because I know that with you, God, all things are possible.

For I know my plans for you declares the LORD, plans to prosper you and not harm you, plans to give you hope and a future. - Jeremiah 29:11

If what you see is all you see, then you do not see all there is to be seen.

Dr. Tony Evans

The Puppet Master

"Aziel, you need to unpack all the boxes in your room before you go to bed!" his mother called from the kitchen. He sighed deeply, glancing at the pile of unpacked boxes in his room.

He stepped out of his bedroom with a mischievous grin. "Mom, do you really want me to unpack all the boxes before I go to bed? I know you don't want your son to look tired and worn out on the first day of his new high school. What kind of first impression would that make?" His voice dripped with sarcasm. He laughed, trying to lighten the mood.

His mother stifled a giggle and cleared her throat, adopting a more serious tone. "Well, you need to put your clothes away at least," she replied, her voice firm but affectionate.

He raised his fist in mock victory. "Yes, ma'am!" he exclaimed, his tone playful yet respectful.

As he returned to his room, he couldn't help but smile. His mom always knew how to balance discipline with love.

Aziel opened the small closet, his thoughts drifting back to his old bedroom in what he now called his dad's place. His current bedroom could fit inside his old one. He referred to it as his dad's place because it no longer felt like home. His father had urged him to stay, hoping to avoid the disruption of changing schools and to allow him to graduate alongside his friends. However, his father didn't grasp that the divorce had already inflicted the most unwelcome change. Staying with his dad would have meant attending the same school with familiar friends and sleeping in a bed he knew, but it also meant living in a house filled with the unfamiliar presence of a divided family.

He yearned for the heartfelt conversations and shared laughter over dinners that once filled their home. He thought about the movies they watched together on Friday nights, smiling as memories of laughter and the smell of buttered popcorn filled his mind. He missed their family trips to church, but his dad had stopped attending and had taken up drinking instead. Aziel remembered how things had worsened after his father's lucrative promotion. He recalled that it marked the beginning of everything falling apart.

He sighed and closed the closet door. The room felt even smaller now, the weight of his memories pressing on him. He longed for the days when his family was whole, and his home was filled with warmth and love. Now, it stood as a constant reminder of what he had lost.

However, his mother never ceased seeking God for solutions and worship, embracing the responsibility of teaching him about God through the Bible. He often heard her reminding his father that teaching their son about God should be led by him. He remembered his father's dismissive smirk and sarcastic comment: "You do such a wonderful job—why change?"

On the other hand, his father introduced him to worldly ways that contradicted God's teachings. His father considered it normal cultural behavior. Aziel still heard his father's words, dripping with disdain for his mother's faith: "There's nothing wrong with pursuing your happiness. Your mother is always ranting about putting God first. My truth is that if you acknowledge God occasionally, you're not ignoring him—he's being included in your life.

Enjoy your life. Follow these basic moral rules, and you'll be fine. Don't rape, steal, kill, or do drugs. Everyone lies and cusses. We're not perfect, so don't try to be perfect. Just respect your mother and me and follow our rules."

Aziel felt a tug of war between his parents' teachings.

He vividly remembered one of the many hurtful arguments between his parents about beliefs and values. His father had come home late, reeking of alcohol, and immediately started criticizing Aziel's mother for constantly seeking God's advice through the Bible and prayer. He insisted it was a waste of time, and that God did not have the answers to improve their life or relationship.

"Look around you," his father said, gesturing broadly to the opulent surroundings of their home. "Do you think we'd have all these nice things if we relied solely on God? No. It takes hard work and long hours to achieve this kind of lifestyle. Do you think God is going to fix our marriage?" his father shouted, his voice slurred. "Once again, the answer is no. You're seeking advice from an outdated book with outdated practices. We need real-time solutions!"

Aziel's mother, trying to remain calm, responded with a befuddled look, "Who are you? When did you allow greed to consume you? If you reflect on the Bible, you'll realize that while times have changed, people and their situations have not. God's word is timeless, offering truth, counsel, and discipline rooted in love. It provides wisdom, strength, and hope when we apply its teachings rather than just read them." She stepped close to him, looking him in his eyes, and put one hand over his heart. "You know the truth, yet you've chosen to remove it from your heart, allowing the desires of the flesh to control you, along with the deceptive whispers of Satan that sound like your own voice. You've fallen for his ultimate deception—questioning God's truth." She sadly sighed, lowering her head. "I miss your true love for me, God, and your son. I have always been grateful for your hard work and how you never prioritized material gain over family. I don't need a big house to make our marriage work. I need the man I knew. You, I don't recognize."

For a moment, she saw his face soften. Then, a sudden chill from her truth ran down his spine, snapping him out of his trance. He shook his head, stepped back from her touch, sucked his teeth, and then laughed bitterly. "Yeah, right, woman. You don't appreciate what I do for you and this family." His voice dripped with sarcasm. "The Bible is your truth. I know my truth. God's Word may give you hope and strength, but not me anymore! I'm doing things my way. You're brainwashing our son with all this nonsense!" His voice grew louder and more agitated. "He must learn to do whatever it takes to make lots of money for true happiness and success!"

His response saddened her. "Is the love of money the only love you find relevant enough to know now?" she said, her voice trembling with emotion. "You talk about REAL-TIME solutions. How have your so-called REAL-TIME solutions worked for us, for you, and our son? Is the over-consumption of alcohol, coming home late, greed, and cursing your wife providing REAL-TIME solutions? Is this the example you want Aziel to follow?"

She paused, taking a deep breath before continuing. "God gives you free will to choose, and you have chosen self-reliance for self-gratification. You have shut God out and allowed the devil in. Look at yourself. Your delusional chase for happiness has torn you apart, along with our family. Your actions are no longer in alignment with Christ. Before your discontentment, our family life was good. We followed the principles from the Bible, which you now refer to as an 'outdated book,' and those principles held our marriage and family together. You are only suffering from the consequences of your choices?" Her tone was sharp and unwavering.

His father's face twisted in anger, but behind it lay a deep-seated pain and regret he never expressed. He had traded his relationship with God and his family for wealth, believing that material success would fulfill him. Unlike before, instead of seeking solace from the Lord God, he found it in a drink and the misguided truths of bad company. Once seen as a blessing, the promotion became a source of immense stress. The long hours and tremendous pressure took their toll, and his nightly ritual of drinking became a misguided attempt to unwind and escape the mounting pressure and anxiety.

As he distanced himself from God, he also distanced himself from his family. The spiritual void in his life amplified his feelings of inadequacy and failure. A growing sense of resentment replaced the warmth of home. Instead of addressing these internal struggles, he buried them under layers of alcohol and bitterness, leading to the destructive behavior that fractured his family. His wife had exposed his inner turmoil, but his drunken pride, fueled by the whispers of dark spirits, prevented him from admitting it. He could hear the sinister voices echoing and laughing, "Leave her. She does not love you," driving him to hold his ears in a desperate attempt to shut them out. Suddenly, Aziel heard his father roar, "I can't do this anymore. I want a divorce," followed by a chair crashing to the floor. His father stormed out of the house, slamming the door behind him with a resounding thud.

Aziel's mother collapsed to the floor, her quiet sobs filling the now-silent room. A whirlwind of emotions swirled within him as he sat frozen in his room—anger, sadness, and a profound sense of helplessness. Gathering his strength, he stood up and cautiously approached his mother's side.

He knelt beside her, gently wrapping his arms around her, offering the same comfort she had always provided him. "Mom, don't cry. I'm always with you, even if Dad decides not to be," he whispered, his voice soft yet filled with resolve.

His mother looked up, her tear-streaked face softening as his words sank in. A small, hopeful smile began to form on her lips, a glimmer of light breaking through the sorrow. The warmth of his embrace and the sincerity in his voice brought a sense of solace she desperately needed. Together, they found peace amid the chaos, bringing them closer together.

His father's words echoed in his mind, dripping with hypocrisy. He demanded obedience and respect, yet his actions were anything but respectable. Aziel felt a deep sense of betrayal. How could his father preach one thing and practice another?

Caught in the crossfire of his parents' conflicting teachings, Aziel felt torn. His mother had taught him the values of God's word, connecting him to Jesus and nurturing his spirit. These teachings resonated deeply within him, offering a sense of peace and purpose. On the other hand, his father's influence had led him down a path of selfish indulgence, practices that brought fleeting pleasure but stood in stark contrast to the divine laws he had known but not always applied.

Aziel's heart ached under the weight of his internal battle. He knew he had to choose between the world's transient pleasures and the eternal truths of his faith. He yearned for the unity and love he once saw between his parents—a bond now shattered and reduced to a permanent separation, sealed by the cold finality of two signatures on a divorce decree. The frequent, hurtful arguments had been heart-wrenching, each chipping away at his family's foundation. He loved his father but had lost respect for him. Aziel decided that home was wherever his mother was, even if it meant downsizing and graduating from a new school.

He knew his mother wasn't perfect, but she always strived to be good and do good. He admired her deeply and fought to imitate her behavior through his emotional struggles rather than following in his father's footsteps. His mother's unwavering strength and kindness were his guiding lights in the storm of his life.

His loss and longing for his old house and its memories were palpable. His emotions were raw and intense, his heart heavy with the weight of change. The familiar walls that once echoed with laughter now felt like distant memories, replaced by an uncertain future.

Amidst the turmoil, Aziel clung to the hope that he could find solace and strength in the values his mother had instilled in him. However, his anger toward his father lingered, preventing him from finding forgiveness or coming to terms with his feelings. He buried these emotions deep within, moving through each day without giving them more thought than necessary.

With a heavy sigh, he began sorting through the boxes. He had to admit that his new home's lofty ceilings were impressive. He only wished he had those innovative hangers his mom had given him to make more space in his closet. He'd never used them because his bedroom closet at his dad's place was so big. He remembered tossing the gadgets somewhere, thinking they were thoughtful gifts but useless.

As he unpacked his regular hangers, he stumbled upon the space-saving gadgets. They had a sticky note attached, reading: "I thought you might need these," accompanied by a couple of heart emojis. Aziel smiled. *Mom always knows.*

After putting his clothes away, he emptied more boxes. He smiled at his progress, knowing his mother would be pleased.

The room filled with unpacked boxes had dwindled to just a few. Among them, one box caught his eye—marked "Azi." A smile spread across his face as he carefully lifted out a handmade wooden box. Sitting on the edge of the bed, he admired the marionette inside, its caramel-colored wood stain gleaming softly. The marionette had hazel eyes and loose curly hair, making it seem almost alive. It wore a matching hoodie, lounge pants, and hand-painted sneakers. Aziel gently ran his fingers along the strings, feeling connected. He closed the box and placed it reverently on his desk.

Art had always been his sanctuary, where he could escape his detrimental thoughts and channel his negative emotions. His gaze drifted to the trophy on top of the bookcase, a proud reminder of his achievement in creating Azi, his self-portrait marionette. But the joy of that accomplishment was overshadowed by the turmoil of his parent's divorce and the upheaval of moving to a new place. Overwhelmed by his thoughts and feelings, he struggled to pick up his sketch pad, which now lay abandoned, collecting dust—a silent testament to his struggle with change and self-identity.

It was getting late. Aziel stood before his standing mirror, holding different outfits against himself and pondering, "What will I wear?" He carefully examined each option, turning slightly to catch different angles. As a senior in a new school, he had to make sure he looked cool. He ran his fingers through his curly, tapered afro, a small smile tugging at his lips as he imagined making a great first impression.

Arriving at school, Aziel glanced at his class schedule. He maintained his composure, not wanting to appear troubled on the morning of his first day at the new school. Quietly, he mouthed his room number, committing it to memory. The unfamiliar surroundings heightened his anxiety, each hallway and classroom a reminder of the fresh start he was about to make. His heart pounded in his chest as he glanced around.

He clutched the strap of his backpack across his slender shoulder as he wandered around the base of the stairs. Was his class on the second floor or the first? Frustration began to settle in. He had no clue where to go.

"Please, God, just a little help. I don't want to look like a lost idiot," he muttered. He shook his head, thinking God had more important things to worry about than his class schedule. Starting up the stairs, he hesitated, then backed down. He was determined to make it to class on time and avoid walking in after the bell rang.

Students passed and bumped into him as if he were invisible. He considered asking someone for help, but everyone seemed absorbed in their world.

A well-built student in a white athletic suit approached and tapped him on the shoulder. Aziel looked up, meeting the student's eyes.

"Dude, are you lost?" the student asked. Aziel smiled and hung his head, embarrassed to confirm it. Navigating a new school was overwhelming, leaving him feeling out of place. His confidence waned with each passing moment, exposing his vulnerability to unfamiliar surroundings.

"Is it written on my forehead?" Aziel asked.

"Clearly," the student laughed. "Are you a freshman or a newbie?"

"A newbie. What's up? I'm Aziel," he replied, holding his fist for the student to bump.

"Nice to meet you. I'm your guardian angel, Jordan," the student snickered and bumped Aziel's fist. Jordan's friendly approach instantly made Aziel feel more at ease.

"Looks like you are. Thanks a lot, man."

"No problem. Let me see your schedule."

Aziel pulled the schedule from his hoodie pocket and handed it to Jordan, who glanced over it.

"Well, your first class is on the second floor."

The two of them moved together at a quick pace. While walking, Jordan pointed out directions to Aziel's other classes. Aziel was grateful for his guidance. The first bell rang just as Jordan stopped.

"Here's your first class. I'll see you around," Jordan shouted as he hurried off.

"Thanks again, Jordan!" Aziel called after him. Jordan threw up his hand in acknowledgment without looking back. Aziel felt a sense of accomplishment for making it to his first class on time, thanks to Jordan's help.

During lunch, Aziel decided to check out the student lounge. He took a seat on a small corner couch, pulling out his morning devotional book. His mother encouraged him to start each day with it, promising it would inspire him. He had to admit that sometimes, God's words seemed perfectly timed to impact his troubled thoughts.

Just as he turned to the page for the day, he heard snickering. Glancing up, he caught the mocking looks of a couple of passing students. Embarrassed, Aziel quickly shoved the small book into his backpack and left the lounge.

On the bus ride home, Aziel replayed his day. He felt he hadn't had a chance to enjoy his new school. He'd gotten lost, been laughed at, and made no potential friends. But then he remembered Jordan—the remarkable student who had helped him. Aziel smiled to himself. Maybe the day wasn't so bad after all.

When he got home, his mother, who worked from home, met him at the door with an anxious smile. She hugged him, eager to hear about his first day.

"Well, how was it?" she asked, her voice filled with curiosity.

Aziel sighed and dropped his shoulders. "It was okay— a typical first day at a new school. I'm drained and want to go to my room. Is that okay?"

She nodded, offering a warm smile. "Of course, son. I saved dinner for you in the fridge if you're hungry," she said as she walked down the hallway toward her home office. "Was your day that bad?" she muttered under her breath, more to herself than to him.

Aziel trudged to his room, dropped his backpack onto the floor with a thud, and crashed onto his bed. He stared at the ceiling, his mind racing. *Was moving here a mistake?* He wondered. But he quickly decided not to let one day define his feelings about the move.

Determined to unwind, he grabbed his earbuds and pulled out his phone. He knew his mother disapproved of the videos and music he enjoyed, but what she found indecent, he found hilarious and soothing. On the other hand, his now-changed father no longer corrected him about his media choices, reminding him that it was just entertainment and no big deal.

Aziel allowed the familiar sounds of his favorite videos and music to wash over him, providing a much-needed escape from the events of his school day. As he lay there, he felt a slight sense of comfort, knowing that tomorrow was a new day filled with new possibilities.

The following day, Aziel hurriedly grabbed his backpack, his movements rushed and frantic. As he swung it over his shoulder, his books tumbled to the floor.

"Are you kidding me?" he muttered, hastily stuffing the books into his bag. One book remained on the floor—his devotional.

Memories of ridicule and embarrassment flooded his mind as he stared at it. His thoughts swirled in a whirlwind of conflicting emotions. He dismissively tossed the devotional onto his bed and dashed toward the front door.

"Aziel," his mom called out, her voice echoing through the hallway.

"I don't want to miss the bus. I love you!" Aziel shouted over his shoulder.

His mother walked into the empty living room, shaking her head before retreating to her office. "Okay, day two," she muttered to herself.

Aziel, now slightly more familiar with his surroundings, skipped lunch again to explore the campus. He wandered to a pavilion near a duck pond, seeking solitude.

After a few moments, an athletically built student approached him. Aziel smiled and waved.

"Hey, I'm Aziel."

"You mean Bible boy?" the student replied sharply, a scornful smile spreading across his face.

Aziel's smile faded, replaced by confusion. He raised an eyebrow. "Excuse me?"

"I saw you in the student lounge reading your Bible," the student mocked.

Aziel felt a flush of embarrassment and shrugged with a nervous laugh. "It's a devotional my mom makes me read."

"So, you're a momma's boy?"

Offended, Aziel stood up. "Look, I don't know you, and you don't know me. I don't want any trouble."

"Then you probably should have stayed sitting, momma's boy."

Aziel clenched his fists, his frustration building. The student shoved him, sending him sprawling to the pavilion floor. His arm scraped against the edge of the bench as he fell.

Wincing in pain, Aziel wrestled to his feet, preparing to defend himself. Just as he was about to swing, he heard someone call his name.

Both Aziel and the student turned toward the voice. Jordan stood a few feet away, his gaze hard and unwavering.

"Back down, Gideon," Jordan said firmly.

Gideon squared his shoulders, meeting Jordan's stare with equal intensity. The student broke the stare and gave Jordan a sinister smile, sucking his teeth. "Nobody calls me Gideon around here, Jordan. I'll see you around," he sneered, bumping his shoulder roughly against Jordan's as he walked away.

Jordan turned to Aziel and helped him to his feet. "Dude, are you okay?"

Aziel looked at the blood-tinged scrape on his arm. "Yeah, I'm okay. This kid just came out of nowhere and started picking a fight with me."

"Do you know him?" Aziel asked.

Jordan nodded. "Yeah, I know him."

"Whatever. What's his problem?"

Jordan shrugged. "Unfortunately, hurt people hurt other people."

Aziel groaned, grabbing his backpack. "This is my second day at this school, and it's not exactly winning me over."

Jordan offered a reassuring smile. "Sorry about that, Aziel. Hey, I'm cool, right?" he said, pointing to himself.

Aziel's lips curved into a small smile. "Yeah, you're the only cool person in this school. Well, the teachers aren't bad. I witnessed a couple of fights today—not including my own."

Jordan sighed, his expression thoughtful. "I focus on the good days. When you look for good, you see good. But if you focus on the bad, you'll see bad."

Aziel shrugged and walked ahead of Jordan. "Maybe you're right. Maybe I've been too focused on the bad to notice the good."

Jordan stopped and watched as Aziel walked away, sensing his sadness.

"There's always good to be seen and something to be grateful for if you align your thoughts with the good," Jordan called out.

Aziel turned and walked backward, facing Jordan. "Dude, you're a saint, but it's hard not to focus on the bad when it feels like it keeps surrounding you," he said, flashing a grin that didn't quite reach his eyes.

His voice wavered slightly, betraying the inner turmoil he was trying to hide. Turning back around, he waved without looking, his steps faltering slightly before disappearing into the crowd.

At home, he saw his mother sitting at the kitchen table, waiting for him. She smiled.

"You are not getting away from me today. Wash your hands. I made your favorite casserole. I want to hear all about your day."

Aziel sighed. The weight of the day's events was still heavy on his shoulders. He wanted to avoid a conversation with his mother once again. He sighed and quickly washed his hands. Kissing her on the head, he sat across from her.

"So, tell me," his mom said anxiously.

Aziel sighed. "Mom, it is only the second day. My classes are good. I am getting familiar with where everything is."

"Are the kids friendly?"

He smiled at her. "Mom, it is high school. Everyone is about themselves."

She raised one eyebrow. "Everybody?"

Aziel shrugged off her question. "There was one kid who helped me out a lot. He is cool."

Aziel reached over to scoop up some of the casserole when his mother noticed the scrape on his arm. Her eyes narrowed with concern.

"What happened to your arm?"

Aziel's heart quickened. Did he want to tell his mother that he had gotten into a fight on the second day of school?

No, he could not tell her the truth. She would worry. Aziel laughed.

"It is so embarrassing. I was running to make it to class on time but fell."

"Oh no. Does it hurt?" Aziel's mother asked, her voice laced with concern. She gently touched his arm, her eyes searching for any signs of pain.

Aziel shook his head. "No."

"Mom, this casserole is good," he said, quickly changing the subject. "Now, tell me about your day."

She smiled softly, understanding his need to divert the conversation. "Thank you, sweetheart. I am glad you like it." She then humored him by talking about her workday and other events, her eyes still occasionally glancing at him with a mix of worry and love.

After eating dinner and showering late, Aziel took out his game controller and headset, eager to dive into his favorite games. He plopped onto his bed. He became involved in the game, laughing and cursing with other gamers online. About twenty minutes into the game, the television screen went blank.

"What?" he exclaimed, throwing the controller onto the bed.

He inspected the television and game console, confirming that everything connected had power. He sighed in frustration. It had to be the controller.

Aziel rummaged through the boxes in his closet to retrieve the spare controller. He pressed the buttons repeatedly, but the game still would not work. Annoyed, Aziel flung himself onto the bed, throwing the controller to the floor.

He sighed deeply and reached for the box that held Azi. He took Azi out of the box and sighed. He began moving the bars of the marionette, making its arms and legs move. Aziel started to talk to Azi. He would engage in a conversation with him from time to time about his thoughts and emotions because he knew Azi could not question or judge him.

"What's happening, Azi? It has been a rough couple of days for me. It must be nice not to have to deal with any bull." He was about to complete the sentence when Azi began to speak.

"Dude, what's up with the potty mouth?"

Aziel threw the marionette to the floor and quickly rolled to the opposite side of the bed.

"I thought we were friends. What kind of friend throws another to the floor?"

Aziel peeped over the bed. "You have lost it. You hear voices that you think are coming from a wooden toy."

"Hey, over here, Aziel!" Azi called out, waving his tiny hands to get Aziel's attention from atop the desk.

"You are not crazy," Aziel muttered, trying desperately to convince himself.

"Are you trying to convince yourself or ask me for confirmation?" The marionette laughed, a whimsical sound that felt comforting and eerie.

Azi strolled to the edge of the desk and casually sat with its legs crossed.

"This is not happening. This is impossible," Aziel muttered again, his voice trembling with disbelief.

"With God, all things are possible," Azi replied.

Aziel blinked in confusion. "I believe in God, but what does God have to do with this delusion?"

The marionette raised one eyebrow. "I am not a delusion. It is because of God that you are now witnessing the supernatural. It is a privilege."

The puppet motioned with its hands. "Come closer; we have much to talk about."

Aziel shook his head in disbelief. "I don't think I am seeing anything supernatural. I am witnessing stress and a mental breakdown. Right now, a puppet with strings is talking and telling me what to do. You are the toy. I control you."

The marionette crossed its arms and raised an eyebrow, its lips curling into a smirk. “Oh? Like how you are controlling me now?” it drawled, its voice dripping with sarcasm.

Aziel's eyes narrowed. He got up from the floor and stomped toward it. “Enough of this. It’s back in the box for you, buddy.”

Upon approaching Azi, a bright glow filled the room. Aziel’s hands shuddered as he covered his eyes, falling to his knees.

When the glow disappeared, Aziel peered through his fingers. Slowly, he removed his hands to focus on the image before him. His jaw dropped, and his eyes widened as if a jolt of electricity surged through his body, leaving him momentarily stunned. In his gaming chair, Jordan smiled, wearing a white jogger suit and holding up Azi in one hand before placing him back on the desk.

"Bro, are you okay? You don’t look so good. That may have been a bad joke, but I couldn’t help myself," Jordan snickered, offering Aziel a hand.

Aziel stared at Jordan's hand momentarily, still trying to process what had just happened.

Jordan pulled Aziel to his feet. Aziel remained standing as Jordan again took his seat.

"Jordan, is that you?" Aziel stammered over his words.

Jordan smiled, nodding his head. "Yes, it's me."

"Jordan, what, how, why? This is impossible."

Jordan sat straight up. "Did I not tell you that nothing is impossible with God?"

"What are you?" Aziel asked with a confused look.

"I am a warrior angel sent by my Lord Jesus Christ at your request for help."

Aziel plopped onto his bed, baffled, with his shoulders slumped. "I thought you were making a joke when you told me you were my guardian angel."

"My apologies. My sarcasm gets me in trouble from time to time. I told you the truth," Jordan laughed.

Aziel suddenly looked at the door and wondered, If I called out to my mom, she could confirm if this was real or if I was having a mental breakdown.

Jordan tilted his head. "What are you thinking about? Are you thinking about calling out to your mother?"

Jordan shook his head. "No, she will not hear you. She is sleeping. This conversation is between us."

Aziel sat up and met his gaze. "What did you do to my mom?"

"Dude, chill. I am an angel of light, not darkness."

Aziel relaxed. "What kind of angel are you?"

Jordan deeply sighed and began to use hand motions, changing the tone of his voice to a high-pitched, slower, sarcastic manner. "Once again, I am a warrior angel."

Aziel chuckled. "Okay, I get it, smart aleck."

Jordan laughed. "What I meant was, what kind of angel talks like you do and makes jokes?"

Jordan put his finger to his lips in sighed deeply. "How am I supposed to talk? You don't think our creator has a sense of humor? Well, he does."

"Aren't you supposed to be serious and quote the Bible in Hebrew, Greek, or some holy language?" Aziel asked, his brow furrowed.

"Which language?" Jordan replied, his eyes twinkling with curiosity.

"Which language do you know?" Aziel asked with a shrug.

Jordan looked at him seriously and answered, "I know them all. I even know your slang. It serves its purpose. I have fun with it, but always with respect."

Jordan shifted his focus to the marionette. "I like your creation of Azi. Is it your likeness it represents?"

Aziel confirmed with a nod.

"Thanks. It took me some time to complete it."

Jordan leaned closer, studying the marionette intently. Without taking his eyes off it, he asked, "Azi is a portrait marionette of you, right?"

Aziel gave a confirming nod.

"Your eyes are a deep brown, but Azi's are hazel. Your curls are tighter, whereas Azi's are looser and longer. Why the difference?"

Aziel shrugged. "I liked those features better."

"On Azi or yourself?" Jordan pressed further.

Aziel lowered his head. "What difference does it make?"

Jordan's gaze sharpened, pinning Aziel with its intensity. "You talk to the marionette because it will not criticize or tell you if you are wrong. You gave it your looks because, in this way, it gives you an illusion of power and control over yourself that you do not have. Am I right?" He tilted his head slightly, his face filled with seriousness.

Aziel's mouth dropped open, eyes widening at the unveiled truth. Unprepared to confront it, annoyance flickered across his face, furrowing his brow.

Jordan raised an eyebrow. "Why are you angry?"

"I don't want to talk about this now," Aziel said, shaking his head.

With a sigh, Jordan leaned back and began to speak in a language that sounded ancient and mystical. "It is written, for we do not wrestle against flesh and blood, but against the rulers, against the authorities, against the cosmic powers over this present darkness, against the spiritual forces of evil in the heavenly places."

Aziel's puzzlement was evident. "What did you just say? What language is that?"

Jordan chuckled softly. "I thought you wanted me to speak a holy language."

Aziel's laughter echoed, easing the tension. Jordan then translated. "That was Aramaic."

"Did you just quote the Bible?" Aziel asked, his eyebrows raised.

Jordan nodded. "Are you familiar with the passage?"

Aziel nodded back. "Yes, I am."

Jordan's expression turned serious. "Aziel, if the Lord allows you to see me, then you know the spiritual battle is real." Holding up two fingers, he continued, "There are two spiritual battles you are involved in: one external, one internal."

Aziel straightened, alert. "Explain."

Jordan's relief was noticeable as he saw that he had Aziel's attention. "The external battle is against evil forces—Satan and his fallen angels. Since the beginning, I've witnessed this spiritual battle from heaven to earth, following the Lord God's commands to aid humans. Though this conflict is mostly unseen, its effects are profoundly evident.

These forces often manifest through corrupt authorities and rulers, who misuse their power to perpetuate injustice and evil in the world."

He paused, then continued, "The internal battle is against the negative influences, thoughts, or behaviors that dictate your actions and decisions. These originate from the flesh, which goes against the spirit. Some of these actions are greed, envy, self-loathing, lust, sexual immorality, hatred, uncontrolled anger, drunkenness, idolatry, sorcery, unforgiveness, and more. Just as we face cosmic forces in the external realm, we must confront these internal struggles equally."

Jordan waved his hand, bringing the marionette to life. "Look at Azi. It is bound and moved by its strings, just as the desires of the flesh bind and move you," he explained, his voice steady and filled with empathy. The marionette's arms and legs moved in different directions. Aziel watched in astonishment.

"You're saying I'm a puppet?"

Jordan nodded. "In many ways, yes. You can control and move Azi in whatever direction you want. Your flesh creates thoughts and desires that steer you towards what it wants, making you believe you are in control because these desires come from within you. But the flesh is pulling your strings. You find yourself walking under its control like a puppet. Satan influences these thoughts of suggestions, making them sound like your own voice through manipulation. When you lose this control because you have given power to the flesh and not the Spirit, you leave Jesus out and invite the devil in. I can tell you Aziel, that Satan will not win this battle."

Aziel scoffed. "It seems like he is winning when you look at all the chaos in the world today."

Jordan smiled gently. "If what you see is all you see, then you do not see all there is to be seen. I told you before. Just like the world, you focus too much on unwelcome news. Try focusing on the good. Trust me, he cannot win. Because he cannot win, he wants to take as many people with him to eternal darkness as he can.

Remember, misery loves company. He manipulates the media to lead you astray, enticing you to indulge in your fleshly desires under the guise of entertainment. This manipulation spans across various forms of media, including people, books, movies, and especially music."

Jordan paused, his gaze piercing into Aziel's soul. "For example, I see people tethered to their electronic devices as if they were their source. Don't get me wrong, these tools can be used for good and to serve God, not replace Him. But I've observed many people, waking by grace, who immediately reach for their device instead of acknowledging their heavenly Father, who, by grace, has given them life to be able to do so."

Aziel averted his eyes, pretending Jordan wasn't referring to him. Jordan cleared his throat and glanced at the ceiling, saying sarcastically, "I didn't mention any names, Aziel." Aziel, feeling nothing but embarrassment, covered his smile. Jordan, sternly looking at him, responded, "I was not joking." Aziel's smile faded. He bit his lip, feeling a mix of shame and anger. His eyes met Jordan's, but he quickly looked away, unable to hold the gaze. Jordan continued.

"Satan, once a mighty angel of light called Lucifer, was given the gift of creating beautiful music in the heavenly realms for worship to GOD. However, after his fall from grace, he has taken this gift to sow chaos and discord on Earth. Satan uses it for his worship of darkness, seeking to pull you away from God and closer to him. He harnesses the energy from provocative music to make you feel more intense, think negatively, and let loose in negative ways. The world believes they see everything but only focus on what the physical eyes see."

Jordan's tone grew more intense. "I can recall the concert you and your friends attended. I saw you all waving your hands high and singing the profane lyrics to the songs. What you were unable to see, and I could see, was Satan hovering high above you, dark wings outstretched, guiding and instructing the rebel angels to whisper the songs into your hearts, amplifying your negative emotions. Satan subtly implants detrimental music ideas into the minds of musicians, suggesting themes and lyrics that provoke fleshly desires. These suggestions take root in the musicians' hearts, leading them to create songs to share and draw people away from God and toward worldly temptations. Through these cleverly disguised inspirations, Satan orchestrates a symphony of deceit, using music to draw people into worshipping him and contributing to their spiritual downfall. This manipulation strengthens my metaphor of people as puppets, controlled by the strings of their fleshly desires."

Aziel's eyes widened in shock. He could almost see the scene playing out in his mind—the pulsating concert, the hypnotic music, and the unseen spiritual forces behind the scenes. He had never considered how deeply music could influence him or the dark power lurking within its melodies. For a fleeting moment, he reevaluated his choice of games and videos, the realization dawning on him like a chilling revelation.

"Music can be a powerful tool for good or evil," Jordan continued. "What you listen to and let into your heart and mind shapes your thoughts and actions. Satan knows this and uses it to his advantage. Be mindful of what you let in, Aziel. The battle is not just around you but within you. Your choice will determine who you are worshipping."

Jordan sighed deeply. "Take this into your mind and heart: by him, all things were created, in heaven and on earth, visible and invisible, whether thrones, dominions, rulers, or authorities—all things were created through him and for him. It is not the other way around. Jesus is the Lord of lords, King of kings. Yet, out of love and salvation for you, He came to this Earth to sacrifice Himself and be ridiculed and spit upon by the ones He created. It sounds like a bad movie, doesn't it?

But trust me, it has a great ending for all who choose to follow him."

Aziel lowered his head in shame. The truth stung him, making his heart ache.

Aziel retorted, "Yes, but it is still my life, and I have control."

Jordan's face softened; his eyes filled with compassion. “It is written that your life is not your own. God has sovereign authority over our existence and the course of our lives for a greater purpose. You may not agree or understand this because His thoughts are not yours, and His ways are not yours. Aziel, does having control mean with or without God? Let me give you two scenarios—one where you include God and the other where you don’t."

Jordan’s voice turned somber as he painted the picture. “In scenario one, where you include God, you wake up daily with purpose. You seek guidance through prayer and find strength in His word. You lean on God with faith and community for support when challenges arise. You read your daily devotion proudly, regardless of what others think. Your home is filled with love and laughter. You have forgiven your father and live harmoniously, talking and laughing together inside the home you once shared. Even on the rough days, remember that God grants you the courage and strength to persevere with God by your side. You may face challenges, but

His presence offers solace and resilience to overcome any obstacle where you eventually receive eternal life with God."

He paused, letting the image sink in before continuing with a hint of sorrow. "In scenario two, where you exclude God, you wake up feeling lost and unsure of your path. You seek solace in distractions, letting social media and temporary pleasures guide you. You seek the world for truth. You hide your faith to avoid ridicule, and your home is a battleground of unresolved anger and distance. You continue not to speak or forgive your father, and the laughter that once filled your home is a distant memory. You are also not truly happy with your physical features, constantly comparing yourself to others and feeling inadequate. This dissatisfaction affects your confidence and how you interact with others. Seeking transient relationship pleasures in the world excludes eternal life with God. Which scenario is appealing to you?" Aziel's fury erupted. He clenched his fists as anger bubbled to the surface. "I don't want to hear this anymore!"

Jordan's voice softened. "Aziel, I know it is hard to hear, but acknowledging the strings that bind you is the first step to cutting them. Free will is a powerful gift but can also be a heavy burden when misused."

Aziel's gaze dropped to the floor, the weight of Jordan's words pressing down on him. The marionette, Azi, stood silently on the desk, symbolically reflecting Aziel's struggle.

Jordan scooted the chair closer to the bed, his presence radiating compassion and strength. "Only with the help of God will you have the power to break free, Aziel. Choose a path led by your spirit, connected with God, to take control of the fleeting desires of the flesh. Why do you think Satan targets the youth?"

Aziel shrugged, his expression dark and brooding. "Your quest for finding your identity, purpose, and meaning leaves you as open targets for negative manipulation, especially if you have misleading guidance. I know for a fact that manipulation is something that Satan excels at. I aided in casting out him and many of my brethren. Like I said, he is angry and will try to take you down with him by breaking your faith in God by any means necessary."

Jordan leaned in, his eyes full of understanding and resolve. "I see the struggle within you, Aziel. The youth are vulnerable, but they also hold immense potential. Satan targets them because he fears what they could become if they get to know God and fulfill their purpose."

Aziel's shoulders shuddered from a chill. His mind was a whirlwind of conflicted emotions. He was torn between the safety of denial and the painful clarity of truth. He was not ready to let go of his pride, but Jordan's words had planted a seed of doubt that would not easily be ignored.

Aziel's voice became soft with sadness. Tears stung his eyes. He did not lift his head to meet Jordan's gaze. "Jordan, please just go," he muttered.

Standing, Jordan's expression softened even further, his angelic presence radiating sorrow and understanding. As he faded from view, his voice echoed with a firm yet compassionate warning, "Be on alert, Aziel. You are denying the suit of armor that safeguards you in this battle, given to you by Jesus. When you deny my help, you deny the Father's help, who sent me."

After Jordan's exit, the marionette collapsed onto the desk. It startled Aziel.

His heart ached with the weight of Jordan's words, and the room felt emptier than ever as he grappled with the truth and his internal battle.

The realization made him nervous—if Jordan knew all these things, God knew them first.

Doubts flickered in his mind. His anger denied the truth of Jordan's words, which held the key to something he had avoided for too long. But he allowed his pride to become one of the strings that moved him, and he was not ready to break free from it.

A week passed, and Jordan stood tall, invisibly on a cloud, observing the world below. His majestic silver wings, highlighted with streaks of gold, were folded neatly against his gleaming silver and gold armor, which shimmered in the ethereal light—ranked as a high-ranking angel, just one step below the mighty Archangel Michael. Michael, the revered Chief of the heavenly hosts, was Jordan's superior and his mentor, guiding him through the celestial hierarchy and the intricacies of divine warfare.

Below, the battle raged on, a fierce conflict invisible to human eyes, sometimes visible to those who have seen the supernatural. Dark angels, their forms shadowy and menacing, moved among the people, whispering insidious thoughts and sowing seeds of chaos. These evil beings thrived on the turmoil they created, and their influence manifested in the actions of those who succumbed to their suggestive thoughts. Arguments erupted without cause, friendships fractured, and despair took root in the hearts of many, a testament to the intensity of the celestial battle.

Amidst this darkness, Jordan could see his brethren angels engaged in the fight, their forms glowing with divine light. Some were invisible, subtly guiding and protecting those open to the Spirit. Others appeared as strangers, giving words of hope and kindness and encouraging acts of compassion. These angels countered the evil forces, helping people rise above the chaos and connect meaningfully. They inspired moments of unexpected generosity, mended broken relationships, and comforted those in despair.

Jordan continued to scan the world below from the clouds, seeing different situations unfold through ethereal windows. In one window, a middle-aged man sat alone in his room, a bottle of pills trembling in one hand and tears streaming down his face. Shadows crept around him as he rocked back and forth on the edge of his bed, staring at a crumpled photo of him and his young daughter on the floor, his eyes vacant and reflecting deep pain.

A fallen angel hovered beside him, whispering words of despair. "You'll never be happy without her," it hissed. "You can join her and end your suffering. Take the pills. Your daughter is waiting for you." These whispers intensified his sorrow, planting the dangerous idea that taking his own life would reunite him with his daughter. Sobbing heavily, he gripped the bottle of pills tighter, shook them toward the heavens, and yelled out, "Why, God? Why did you take her from me?" His voice was filled with anguish. The dark spirits seized the moment, twisting his grief into a belief that God had abandoned him and that ending his life was the only escape. Jordan's voice and light, filled with divine compassion and authority, cut through the darkness, making the demons flee.

"Your pain is real, but so is God's love for you," he whispered. "Taking your life is not the answer. It is murder. It is written that you shall not murder. God has a purpose for you, even in your grief. He is with you, ready to carry you through this darkness with faith."

He picked up the crumpled photo and held it close to his chest. The man's heart began to calm as Jordan's comforting words pierced through the dark whispers. He realized that his daughter would want him to live, find peace, and continue his life, knowing that God still had a purpose for him. This realization filled him with a sense of peace and hope. He was comforted by the truth that his daughter was back in the hands of the Creator, who had gifted her to him, safe and loved. A small smile pursed his lips.

In another window, a young woman sat alone in her room, her face etched with worry and fear. Her anxiety stemmed from a deep-seated fear of failure, especially in her career. The next day, she had an important presentation, and the thought of standing before her colleagues and possibly making a mistake terrified her.

Dark spirits seized upon this fear, whispering insidious thoughts into her mind. "You're not prepared enough. You'll make a fool of yourself. They'll laugh at you." These suggestions took root, magnifying her insecurities and warping her perception of reality.

The whispers grew louder as she sat at her desk, trying to rehearse. Her detrimental thoughts spun out of control, creating vivid images of her failure. She saw herself stumbling over her words, her colleagues' faces twisted in mockery. The scene became so real in her mind that her heart began to race.

Suddenly, her breathing quickened, and her chest tightened. She clutched at her heart, feeling a panic attack surge through her. The dark spirits' whispers intensified, amplifying her sense of hopelessness. Her world spun out of control as the panic attack took hold, leaving her gasping for air and feeling utterly alone.

Jordan's heart ached as he watched her struggle. Her thoughts were clouded by a lack of understanding and misconceptions about what it truly meant to seek God's guidance. She believed she had to navigate her pain and anxiety alone, relying solely on her fleshly guidance rather than including God's guidance. Jordan knew that if she could recognize the source of these thoughts and turn to God for strength, she could break free from the chains of anxiety.

Yet, in another window, Jordan saw a group of believers praying. Their faces were illuminated with divine light, and good angels surrounded them, shielding them from the dark spirits. The believers' faith functioned as a powerful barrier, inspiring hope and protecting them from the chaos that sought to invade their hearts and minds.

Upon God's command, Jordan's resolve hardened. He knew his mission was urgent and crucial. He was to fight the dark forces, protect the believers, and bind the dark spirits that plagued them. He drew his celestial sword with a mighty roar, its blade gleaming with divine light. He descended into the fray, his wings spreading wide as he charged into battle, a sense of urgency and determination driving his every move.

The dark angels recoiled at his approach, their shadowy forms flickering in the presence of his holy light. Jordan's sword, a manifestation of divine justice, gleamed with a brilliance that pierced the very fabric of the darkness. He moved with the grace and power of a seasoned warrior, striking down the dark spirits with precision. Each swing of his sword sent waves of light rippling through the darkness, binding the dark angels and casting them into the abyss.

Upon returning to the cloud above Aziel's school, the memory of the last conversation between him and Aziel lingered, a constant reminder of his failure to reach him with the truth. As he scanned the campus below, his eyes caught a glimpse of Aziel walking among the students. A familiar fallen angel, its form a grotesque distortion of angelic beauty, approached Aziel. Its wings, once radiant, were now tattered and blackened, and its eyes, once filled with light, now glowed with an evil fire. The fallen angel leaned in to whisper its malevolent thoughts. It caught sight of Jordan and flashed a menacing smile. "Gideon," Jordan mumbled through clenched teeth.

Aziel's expression changed, his eyes darkening as he accepted the thoughts as his own. Jordan's heart pounded as he watched the fallen angel merge with Aziel, its influence taking hold. Jordan readily reached for his sword. He was ready to descend and save Aziel, but a powerful, commanding voice stopped him.

"Jordan, stand down."

God's firm command was given with compassion. "I know you want to help, but it is Aziel's free will that I do not intervene."

Jordan's hand fell away from his sword. He could only watch with sorrow as Aziel walked away.

Jordan watched in dismay as Aziel's demeanor grew increasingly aggressive. His new friends were corrupt and of a bad influence. Jordan shook his head as he saw Aziel's new associates egg him on to bully another student. He stuck his foot out and tripped the student. The group erupted in laughter as the student fell, his eyes narrowing in anger, his face flushed with embarrassment. Aziel's smirk remained even as the fallen student lunged at him, tackling him to the ground. A crowd of students quickly gathered, shouting and recording the fight on their phones. His newfound friends left him to fight for himself. Aziel managed to land a punch to the student's mouth, drawing blood before a security guard intervened, pulling them apart and leading them to the office.

He slumped into a chair in front of the principal's desk. "Well, hello Aziel. This isn't how I like to get to know my students," she said, flashing a warm smile that revealed her left dimple. She brushed a stray curl from her eye and focused on his file. "You're new here. What's the problem? Do you not like our school?"

He shrugged, avoiding eye contact.

"Aziel, look at me. I asked you a question." The principal's voice was stern, her eyes fixed on him.

He raised his voice. "I gave you an answer."

The principal's eyebrows shot up at his disrespect. "No, you didn't."

Aziel straightened up, lowering his voice. "No, I don't like this school," he said, a sinister smile creeping onto his lips.

"Hmmm," she murmured, flipping through his file without looking at him. "I spoke with your mother. She seems like a nice woman, but she is extremely disappointed in your behavior," she said, clicking her tongue in disapproval. She handed him the referral, saying, "You are suspended for three days. You can go."

Aziel snatched the referral with a scowl and stormed out of the office. Outside, he stuffed the referral inside his bag. As he was about to zip it up, he noticed his devotional lying there.

His brows furrowed, and his eyes darted as if searching for an explanation. He did not remember putting it in his bag. A dark thought crossed his mind: Put the book in the trash. *How is it helping you? You're having a tough time now; how is God helping you?* Aziel became enraged. He grabbed his bag and threw the devotional in the trash.

When Aziel arrived home, he saw his mother sitting on the sofa, waiting with her arms and legs crossed. Her look was stern. He let out an aggravated sigh and began to speak, but his mother cut him short.

"Do not talk. You are grounded. I have taken every electrical device from your room." She held out her hand. "Give me your phone."

Aziel's anger ignited, and he threw his phone against the wall, shattering the screen. "Would you let me talk? Now I know what Dad means when you don't let him talk. Before, I thought it was entirely his fault, but now I see it differently."

His mother's face fell, sadness washing over her. "Well, I would say that your behavior surprises me, but after that statement, it only confirms that the apple does not fall far from the tree. You are your father's son. You should go live with him since you want to copy his unhealthy habits."

Aziel stepped closer, a wicked smile spreading across his face. "Gladly!"

His mother's heart quickened with his approach. She never thought she would witness the day when her son's behavior would make her nervous. She deliberately hurt him with her words because he had hurt her with his. The heartbreak was notable. She hated reacting badly to hurtful behavior, but the cycle had become familiar between her and his father. She did not want to bring the same tumultuous energy into their new lives, which had already painfully broken up their family. Tears sprang to her eyes as Aziel left the room.

Aziel slammed his door shut and flung his backpack onto the floor. The raw emotion in his mother's voice lingered in his mind, adding weight to his steps. With a frustrated sigh, he sat at his desk and shoved his Bible away from him. The room closed around him. His thoughts overwhelmed him, swirling in a storm of confusion and regret. His mother's words stung deeply; they exposed a truth he did not want to face. He realized he was mirroring his father's behavior, making him angry and hurt. But there was something darker, more unfamiliar stirring within him. With all his electronics gone, he was left alone with his turbulent thoughts, the silence amplifying the chaos inside.

The conversation with Jordan suddenly flooded his thoughts. Aziel knew he had only become angry with Jordan because Jordan had revealed the truth, which Aziel had denied. This meant he truthfully rejected the help of Jesus. Jordan was sent to care for him upon his request received by the Lord. Aziel felt ashamed. He disliked his actions but found himself unable to regain control; he was a puppet controlled by the root of darkness and his shortcomings, stemming from his thoughts of the flesh. He missed his friend Jordan and felt sorry for his behavior.

It was getting late, and Aziel decided to take a hot shower. He hoped that a relaxing shower would wash away today's events. Steam enveloped him, providing a temporary sanctuary from his racing thoughts. He felt a fleeting calm as the hot water cascaded over him.

Aziel wiped the fog from the mirror, revealing his reflection. As he cleared the glass, a shadowy figure appeared behind him. His breath quickened, and his heart pounded in his chest. He spun around, but the bathroom was empty. The only sound was the dripping of water from the showerhead.

"Get it together, Aziel," he whispered, trying to shake off the eerie feeling. He quickly dressed and trotted back to his room, his mind racing with fear and confusion.

Aziel climbed into bed, pulling the covers up to his chin. The desk lamp began to flicker, casting eerie shadows on the walls. Aziel sat up, his heart quickening. He glanced at the marionette slumped innocently on his desk. Suddenly, Azi snapped upright, its lifeless face contorting into a menacing grin. Aziel's mouth gaped open as he hid under the covers, shivering. The room felt colder, and the air seemed thicker, as if the atmosphere were charged with an unseen presence. He closed his eyes, trying to convince himself that it was all in his head.

But then, he felt a chilly wind blow through his closed window, rustling the pages of his Bible. Suddenly, the Bible combusted into flames, and ashes swirled around the room.

Aziel's terror spiked. The room plunged into darkness. He leaped from the covers and dashed for the door. He tried to open it, but the handle burned like hot coals, blistering his hand. He screamed, but no sound came from his throat. He yelled for his mother, but no words escaped his lips. He clutched his throat as if trying to pull out the sound of his voice.

Aziel was thrown to the bed by an unseen force. He curled into a protective fetal position, sobbing bitterly. He tried to cry out to Jesus, but no words formed. Desperately, he began to pray in his thoughts, asking the Lord to forgive him earnestly for all his hurtful words, thoughts, and actions. He pleaded for help, his breathing growing shallow and a tightness gripping his chest. The room closed around him as the darkness grew more oppressive.

In the stifling silence, a sinister voice dripping with malice echoed through Aziel's mind. "*You belong to me, Aziel. No one, not even God, can save you from my grasp.*" The demon's voice laughed, a chilling, hollow sound reverberating from every corner of the room. Aziel's heart pounded in his chest as he struggled to hold on to his faith, the malevolent laughter ringing in his ears and threatening to drown out his desperate prayers.

Jordan stood on his post in the heavens, his majestic wings spread abroad, watching and waiting.

Suddenly, a powerful, commanding voice broke the silence of the heavens. It was the voice of God, resonating through the celestial realm with authority and grace. "Jordan," God commanded, "go to Aziel. Release him from Astaroth and throw him into the pit, where he will await my judgment."

He swooped down from the heavens without hesitation, cutting through the darkness like a beacon of light. Standing tall at the foot of Aziel's bed, Jordan said, "Astaroth, come out in the name of our Lord Jesus Christ."

Aziel's body lifted as Astaroth emerged with dark, tattered wings, towering and matching Jordan's height. "You mean your LORD," Astaroth sneered, his voice dripping with malice. Aziel lay motionless, his eyes wide with terror, his body trembling uncontrollably, witnessing the supernatural standoff in his room.

Jordan's eyes narrowed. "Yeah, I'm not here for small talk," he retorted, his tone steely. "I came to drop you off at your new home, Tartarus, where you will await judgment with your other homies."

Astaroth threw his head back and laughed, a chilling sound that echoed through the room. "I don't think so," he said, his form suddenly shooting through the ceiling in a burst of dark energy.

Jordan sighed, a mix of frustration and determination in his breath. "Always the hard way." He looked at Aziel, still clutching the covers in fear and disbelief.

"Aziel, do not be afraid, I will return," he said, his voice filled with comfort, as he quickly followed the fallen angel through the ceiling.

Astaroth rose above the clouds, his dark-handled swords drawn, ready for the impending battle. Jordan met him, unsheathing his majestic swords. The silver blades shimmered. The golden hilts were encrusted with a stunning array of diamonds and precious jewels, symbolizing his second-in-command rank.

Astaroth scoffed, a wicked grin spreading across his face, his eyes burning with jealousy and resentment. His voice dripped with venom as he spat, "Déjà vu, huh, Jordan? Those swords should be mine. Why would Michael choose you over me?"

Jordan sucked his teeth. "Gideon, are you still nursing that old wound? You allow your ego to consume you, just like Satan."

Gideon, now Astaroth, yelled back, "It's Astaroth!"

Jordan smirked. "Whatever you call yourself, I'm here to bring you down."

Astaroth blurted out a laugh filled with the sound of dark satisfaction. "Not this time. This time, I am taking you with me, and you'll be tossed into the pit of my Master, Satan."

Jordan smiled, a light shining in his eyes. "Your master, Satan. Say that aloud to yourself while in the pit of Tartarus, awaiting your judgment from the true Master and Lord, Jesus."

Astaroth's rage surged, and he lunged at Jordan. With swift precision, Jordan landed a powerful kick into Astaroth's chest, sending him flipping clumsily through the air. Astaroth struggled to regain his composure, flailing for a moment before managing to steady himself.

Jordan positioned himself in a battle stance, his swords out in front, waiting. "You do remember how this ended last time," he said calmly.

Astaroth roared and charged at Jordan, their swords clashing with a thunderous impact.

Jordan parried Astaroth's strikes with grace, each movement deliberate and precise. Astaroth, driven by anger, attacked with wild fury, but his movements were erratic and desperate.

Jordan sidestepped and slashed Astaroth's swords into halves with a swift move, sending them plummeting toward the earth. Astaroth's eyes widened in disbelief and anger.

Jordan sheathed his swords. "Your anger consumes you, Astaroth. Once again, you can't win this battle," he said, his voice steady and unwavering.

Astaroth roared again, mustering all his strength for one final assault. He charged at Jordan, but Jordan was ready. He grabbed Astaroth and bound his body with celestial chains. He looked into Astaroth's eyes and said, "You chose the wrong side. God's power and goodness will always prevail." Astaroth thrashed and screamed, but the chains tightened, glowing with a holy light that burned through his darkness.

As he dropped Astaroth into the gaping pit of Tartarus below, he could hear his screams echo as he plummeted into the abyss, mingling with the distant roars of other rebel angels. Jordan watched until the darkness swallowed the sound, then turned away, his mission complete.

Jordan soared back to Aziel to check on him. He heard Aziel being comforted by his mother, his cries filling the room as he apologized. Jordan stood invisibly at the foot of the bed, listening.

"Jordan?" Aziel whispered. His mother asked, "Who is Jordan, honey?"

"Mom, do you believe everything I have told you about what has happened?" Aziel asked, his voice tinged with uncertainty. "Do you believe me about Jordan, my guardian angel?"

“Of course, Aziel,” his mother replied warmly. “I would be a hypocrite to teach you about the supernatural and not believe it myself.” She gently held up his wrapped hand and kissed his wound knowingly. “With God, all things are possible.”

His mother smiled and kissed him on the head. “I also apologize to you, Aziel, for my words.”

“It's okay, Mom. I am going to be a better son. You will see. I am sorry for the trouble I caused.”

“Good night, son. You are a good son.”

"Good night, Momma. Love you."

After his mother closed the door, Jordan appeared, towering over him. The gold and silver in his armor and wings shimmered, and Aziel was in awe. "Wow! I still can't believe seeing you towering over me is like being close to God. He saved me after I rebelled against Him. It is a privilege, and I do not understand why He chose me. I do not deserve His mercy and grace." Aziel became saddened.

Jordan gracefully sat on the floor, transforming into the familiar student Aziel had first met. He was dressed in his white joggers and tennis shoes. Aziel perked up and smiled, comforted by seeing Jordan appear as his friend again.

"Aziel, He heard you ask for forgiveness. He rescued you because He loves you. He allowed you to see the supernatural to witness to others about the God He is, the power He has, and His love for humanity."

Aziel shook his head in agreement. "I am a witness to that Jordan. Again, thank you."

"Don't thank me, thank God. It is all in a day's work for me."

"Well, I'm off, Aziel."

"Wait, what if I need you again?"

Jordan laughed. "The Lord our God is always with you when you are with Him. Call Him, and He will answer." Jordan spoke again in Aramaic: "Whoever is ashamed of me and my words, of him will the Son of Man be ashamed when he comes in his glory and the glory of the Father and the holy angels." Aziel gave him a questionable look. He gave him the translation, and Aziel bowed in shame, recalling how he had hidden his devotion whenever others mocked him.

"Always look for the good and give thanks. Become transformed by renewing your mind, changing negative thinking, and aligning your Spirit with God's, breaking free from the strings of the flesh that keep your thoughts bound. When you start practicing the fruits of the Spirit—love, joy, peace, patience, kindness, goodness, faithfulness, gentleness, and self-control—you will begin to see things from God's perspective and make decisions that honor Him, separating you from the world. Are you ready for separation? Are you prepared to become different?" Jordan emphasized the word different, creating quotation marks with his fingers. "Jesus said when you follow him, it will cause division even in your household. So, be on guard."

When you make friends with the world, it causes enmity with God. Never give up an opportunity to witness what you know and learn about the truth. You will know who your loyal friends are."

Jordan pointed at Aziel. "Oh, one more important thing to remember. Don't forget to show hospitality to strangers. You could be entertaining an angel." Jordan winked with a wide smile.

Aziel laughed. "I will never forget that or any of this. Thanks, man."

Jordan stood up. "This world keeps me busy. I am going to ask my LORD for a Sabbath day." Jordan and Aziel laughed together.

"Jordan, a Sabbath from saving lives? The LORD has His hands full with you and humanity." Jordan shrugged. "What can I say? I am unique. Peace, man," he said, holding up two fingers before disappearing in a bright glow.

Aziel walked over and clicked on the desk lamp. He placed Azi back in the wooden box. He noticed his Bible and devotional book lay on top of each other in perfect condition. Aziel smiled and whispered, "Thank you, Lord, for rescuing me." He brushed his hands across the Bible, knowing his faith would be changed forever.

I hope you enjoyed The Puppet Master. As you reflect on the journey of the characters of truth, consider how the fruits of the Spirit manifest in your own life. Take a moment to meditate on the passages below, which explain and provide practical applications of the fruits of the Spirit. Let these insights inspire you to renew your thoughts and always focus on positive, good thoughts. For more good thoughts to ponder, you can read my blog at www.goodthoughtstoponder.com

Application of the fruits of the Spirit

Practicing the fruit of the Spirit, as described in Galatians 5:22-23, profoundly benefits our lives and relationships. These attributes include love, joy, peace, patience, kindness, goodness, faithfulness, gentleness, and self-control. Here's how cultivating these virtues can transform your life:

Love

Deepens Connections: Expressing genuine love fosters more profound, more meaningful relationships.

Reduces Conflict: Love encourages understanding and forgiveness, helping resolve conflicts peacefully.

Joy

Enhances Well-being: Embracing joy improves mental health and overall well-being.

Attracts Positivity: A joyful attitude attracts positive experiences and relationships.

Peace

Promotes Calmness: Inner peace helps manage stress and anxiety.

Fosters Harmony: Peaceful interactions lead to harmonious relationships and environments.

Patience

Improves Endurance: Patience helps you endure difficult situations with grace.

Encourages Understanding: Being patient with others fosters empathy and better communication.

Kindness

Builds Trust: Acts of kindness build trust and respect in relationships.

Spreads Positivity: Kindness creates a ripple effect, encouraging others to be kind as well.

Goodness

Reflects Integrity: Living with goodness shows integrity and moral character.

Inspires Others: Your actions can inspire others to strive for goodness.

Faithfulness

Strengthens Commitment: Faithfulness in your commitments builds reliability and trustworthiness.

Deepens Relationships: Faith strengthens bonds with family, friends, and community.

Gentleness

Promotes Compassion: Gentleness fosters compassion and understanding.

Reduces Aggression: A gentle approach can defuse conflicts and reduce aggression.

Self-Control

Enhances Discipline: Practicing self-control improves discipline and focus.

Prevents Regret: Exercising self-control helps you make better choices and avoid regretful actions.

Overall Benefits

Spiritual Growth: Cultivating the fruit of the Spirit deepens your relationship with God and enhances spiritual growth.

Improved Relationships: These virtues lead to healthier, more fulfilling relationships with others.

Personal Fulfillment: Living by these principles brings a sense of purpose and fulfillment.

By nurturing these virtues, you align your actions with your faith, positively impacting your life and the lives of those around you. Ready to embrace and practice the fruit of the Spirit?

Galatians 5:18 Explained

In Galatians 5:18, Paul writes, "But if you are led by the Spirit, you are not under the law." This phrase carries significant theological weight and implications.

Meaning and Context

Paul's message in this verse is that the Old Testament law does not bind those guided by the Holy Spirit in the same way as before Christ's sacrifice. Here's a deeper look:

Freedom from the Mosaic Law

The "law" refers to the Mosaic Law, which includes the commandments and regulations given to the Israelites. Being "under the law" meant being obligated to follow these rules to achieve righteousness.

New Covenant through the Spirit

With the coming of Jesus Christ and his sacrificial death and resurrection, believers enter a new covenant with God. Instead of being justified by adherence to the law, believers are justified by faith in Christ and are guided by the Holy Spirit.

Living by the Spirit

When Paul says believers are "led by the Spirit," he means that the Holy Spirit directs and influences their lives. This results in a way of life that naturally fulfills the law's righteous requirements without the need for adherence to a written code.

Grace and Faith

Under this new covenant, believers live by grace and faith rather than strictly observing the law. This doesn't mean lawlessness but rather that their actions are motivated by love and guided by the Spirit, leading to genuine righteousness.

Practical Implications

Inner Transformation: Believers experience an inner transformation as the Holy Spirit works within them, leading to a life that reflects God's will.

Freedom in Christ: This freedom means being liberated from the condemnation that comes with failing to keep the law perfectly. Instead, believers are encouraged to follow the Spirit, which results in a life of love, joy, peace, and other fruits of the Spirit.

Empowerment: The Holy Spirit empowers believers to live in a way that pleases God, not out of obligation but out of a transformed heart and mind.

By being led by the Spirit, believers experience true freedom and the ability to live in a way that honors God, transcending the limitations and condemnations of the old law. It's a profound shift from external adherence to internal transformation.

Living by the Flesh vs. Living by the Spirit

This is crucial in understanding the difference between living under the law and by the Spirit. When we rely on our strength, or the flesh, to achieve victory or motivate God to act, we often fall short and experience frustration.

Living by the Flesh

Relying on our strength, known as living by the flesh, often involves:

Self-Reliance: Trying to achieve righteousness through our efforts and works.

Pride: Believing we can earn God's favor or manipulate His will through our actions.

Frustration: Feeling defeated when we inevitably fall short of the law's demands, leading to guilt and shame.

Biblical Perspective

Paul addresses this in several places in the New Testament:

Romans 8:8: "Those who are in the realm of the flesh cannot please God."

Galatians 3:3: "Are you so foolish? After beginning by means of the Spirit, are you now trying to finish by means of the flesh?"

Self-Reflection Questions

1. What are some of your fleshly desires, and where do they originate?

2. How do you typically respond to these desires?

3. Could you reflect on a time when you successfully resisted a fleshly desire by applying biblical principles?
What was the outcome?

4. How can you cultivate the fruits of the Spirit in your actions and behaviors this week?

5. How can your connection with God be strengthened to help overcome fleshly desires?

6. When you struggle with fleshly desires, do you use self-reliance for solutions or turn to Jesus? What differences do you notice when you choose one over the other?

Scripture References for Reflection

Luke 9:26: ESV "For whoever is ashamed of me and of my words, of him will the Son of Man be ashamed when he comes in his glory and the glory of the Father and of the holy angels."

Galatians 5:17-19 ESV "For the desires of the flesh are against the Spirit, and the desires of the Spirit are against the flesh, for these are opposed to each other, to keep you from doing the things you want to do. But if you are led by the Spirit, you are not under the law. Now the works of the flesh are evident: sexual immorality, impurity, sensuality."

Ephesians 6:12-18 ESV "For we do not wrestle against flesh and blood, but against the rulers, against the authorities, against the cosmic powers over this present darkness, against the spiritual forces of evil in the heavenly places. Therefore, take up the whole armor of God, that you may be able to withstand in the evil day, and having done all, to stand firm. Stand therefore, having fastened on the belt of truth, and having put on the breastplate of righteousness, and, as shoes for your feet, having put on the readiness given by the gospel of peace. In all circumstances, take up the shield of faith, with which you can extinguish all the flaming darts of the evil one; and take the helmet of salvation, and the sword of the Spirit, which is the word of God, praying at all times in the Spirit, with all prayer and supplication. To that end, keep alert with all perseverance, making supplication for all the saints."

Romans 12:2 ESV: "Do not be conformed to this world, but be transformed by the renewal of your mind, that by testing you may discern what is the will of God, what is good and acceptable and perfect."

James 4:4: ESV "You adulterous people! Do you not know that friendship with the world is enmity with God? Therefore, whoever wishes to be a friend of the world makes himself an enemy of God."

2 Corinthians 13:5: ESV "Examine yourselves, to see whether you are in the faith. Test yourselves. Or do you not realize this about yourselves, that Jesus Christ is in you? — unless indeed you fail to meet the test!"

Galatians 5:22-23: ESV "But the fruit of the Spirit is love, joy, peace, forbearance, kindness, goodness, faithfulness, gentleness and self-control. Against such things, there is no law.

Colossians 1:16: ESV "For by him all things were created, in heaven and on earth, visible and invisible, whether thrones or dominions or rulers or authorities—all things were created through him and for him."

Hebrews 13:2: ESV Do not neglect to show hospitality to strangers, for thereby some have entertained angels unawares.

Isaiah 55:8-9 (NIV): For my thoughts are not your thoughts, neither are your ways my ways," declares the LORD. "As the heavens are higher than the earth, so are my ways higher than your ways and my thoughts than your thoughts.

Jeremiah 10:23: NLT: I know, LORD, that our lives are not our own. We are not able to plan our own course.

Jeremiah 29:11 (NIV): "For I know the plans I have for you," declares the LORD, "plans to prosper you and not to harm you, plans to give you hope and a future."

Matthew 10:34-36 (NIV): Do not suppose that I have come to bring peace to the earth. I did not come to bring peace, but a sword. For I have come to turn 'a man against his father, a daughter against her mother, a daughter-in-law against her mother-in-law— a man's enemies will be the members of his own household.

Philippians 4:6-7 (NIV): Do not be anxious about anything, but in every situation, by prayer and petition, with thanksgiving, present your requests to God. And the peace of God, which transcends all understanding, will guard your hearts and your minds in Christ Jesus.

Made in the USA
Columbia, SC
05 April 2025

5784c7b5-1f2c-4575-86d9-b44c0e97e0cbR01